This Anxiety Workbook

Belongs to

____

RULES

Anxiety and depression levels are rapidly rising. Many people turn to write down their feelings to help them manage their mental health and comfort. You will find here some therapeutic techniques.

HAPPY MEMORY CLOUDS PAGES:

Here you can jot down reminders of numerous happy memories.
You can return to these pages whenever you are feeling stressed or anxious.
and elect a memory to bear in mind and meditate upon.
It's like emergency memory jogging time for you.

COMBAT ANXIETY PAGES:

Here you are encouraged to spend some time analyzing a beloved safe space, making notes of emotional cues like aromas, textures, or/and the existence of supportive people and animals. The Combat Anxiety pages can be fictional or real places that they link with peaceful and comforting emotions.

When you are feeling stressed or nervous, you can quickly return to these pages to begin your own visualization and then step temporarily away from the stressful area to a quiet one, where you can meditate calmly and return to yourself.

For questions and any suggestions,
please email us at:

wahasis.books@gmail.com

DATE:

WHAT WERE YOU DOING?

WHERE WERE YOU?

WHO WAS THERE?

COLORS

SMELLS

TEXTURES

TASTES

SOUNDS

FILL OUT THESE CLOUDS AS YOU THINK OF HAPPY MEMORIES. USE THEM WHEN YOUR EMOTIONS BECOME OVERWHELMING.

NOTES

IMAGINATION PAGE

TITLE OF SPACE ____

SKETCH YOUR SAFE SPACE HERE:

WORDS THAT DESCRIBE YOUR SPACE:

SOUNDS

SIGHTS

SMELLS

TEXTURES

PEOPLE AND ANIMALS PRESENT

TITLE OF SPACE --

SKETCH YOUR SAFE SPACE HERE:

WORDS THAT DESCRIBE YOUR SPACE:

SOUNDS

SIGHTS

SMELLS

TEXTURES

PEOPLE AND ANIMALS PRESENT

WHAT WERE YOU DOING?

WHERE WERE YOU?

WHO WAS THERE?

COLORS

SMELLS

TEXTURES

SOUNDS

TASTES

FILL OUT THESE CLOUDS AS YOU THINK OF HAPPY MEMORIES. USE THEM WHEN YOUR EMOTIONS BECOME OVERWHELMING.

NOTES

IMAGINATION PAGE

DATE:

TITLE OF SPACE ....

SKETCH YOUR SAFE SPACE HERE:

WORDS THAT DESCRIBE YOUR SPACE:

SOUNDS

SIGHTS

SMELLS

TEXTURES

PEOPLE AND
ANIMALS PRESENT

TITLE OF SPACE ____

SKETCH YOUR SAFE SPACE HERE:

WORDS THAT DESCRIBE YOUR SPACE:

SOUNDS

SIGHTS

SMELLS

TEXTURES

PEOPLE AND ANIMALS PRESENT

DATE:

WHAT WERE YOU DOING?

WHERE WERE YOU?

WHO WAS THERE?

COLORS

SMELLS

TEXTURES

SOUNDS

TASTES

FILL OUT THESE CLOUDS AS YOU THINK OF HAPPY MEMORIES. USE THEM WHEN YOUR EMOTIONS BECOME OVERWHELMING.

IMAGINATION PAGE

TITLE OF SPACE ....

SKETCH YOUR SAFE SPACE HERE:

WORDS THAT DESCRIBE YOUR SPACE:

SOUNDS

SIGHTS

SMELLS

TEXTURES

PEOPLE AND ANIMALS PRESENT

DATE:

TITLE OF SPACE ____

SKETCH YOUR SAFE SPACE HERE:

WORDS THAT DESCRIBE YOUR SPACE:

SOUNDS

SIGHTS

SMELLS

TEXTURES

PEOPLE AND ANIMALS PRESENT

WHAT WERE YOU DOING?

WHERE WERE YOU?

WHO WAS THERE?

COLORS

SMELLS

TEXTURES

SOUNDS

TASTES

FILL OUT THESE CLOUDS AS YOU THINK OF HAPPY MEMORIES. USE
THEM WHEN YOUR EMOTIONS BECOME OVERWHELMING.

NOTES

IMAGINATION PAGE

DATE:

TITLE OF SPACE ____

SKETCH YOUR SAFE SPACE HERE:

WORDS THAT DESCRIBE YOUR SPACE:

SOUNDS

SIGHTS

SMELLS

TEXTURES

PEOPLE AND ANIMALS PRESENT

TITLE OF SPACE --

SKETCH YOUR SAFE SPACE HERE:

WORDS THAT DESCRIBE YOUR SPACE:

SOUNDS

SIGHTS

SMELLS

TEXTURES

PEOPLE AND ANIMALS PRESENT

DATE:

WHAT WERE YOU DOING?

WHERE WERE YOU?

WHO WAS THERE?

COLORS

SMELLS

TEXTURES

TASTES

SOUNDS

FILL OUT THESE CLOUDS AS YOU THINK OF HAPPY MEMORIES. USE
THEM WHEN YOUR EMOTIONS BECOME OVERWHELMING.

NOTES

IMAGINATION PAGE

TITLE OF SPACE

SKETCH YOUR SAFE SPACE HERE:

WORDS THAT DESCRIBE YOUR SPACE:

SOUNDS

SIGHTS

SMELLS

TEXTURES

PEOPLE AND ANIMALS PRESENT

TITLE OF SPACE --

SKETCH YOUR SAFE SPACE HERE:

WORDS THAT DESCRIBE YOUR SPACE:

SOUNDS

SIGHTS

SMELLS

TEXTURES

PEOPLE AND ANIMALS PRESENT

WHAT WERE YOU DOING?

WHERE WERE YOU?

WHO WAS THERE?

COLORS

SMELLS

TEXTURES

SOUNDS

TASTES

FILL OUT THESE CLOUDS AS YOU THINK OF HAPPY MEMORIES. USE
THEM WHEN YOUR EMOTIONS BECOME OVERWHELMING.

DATE:

TITLE OF SPACE --

SKETCH YOUR SAFE SPACE HERE:

WORDS THAT DESCRIBE YOUR SPACE:

SOUNDS

SIGHTS

SMELLS

TEXTURES

PEOPLE AND ANIMALS PRESENT

DATE:

TITLE OF SPACE --

SKETCH YOUR SAFE SPACE HERE:

WORDS THAT DESCRIBE YOUR SPACE:

SOUNDS

SIGHTS

SMELLS

TEXTURES

PEOPLE AND ANIMALS PRESENT

DATE:

WHAT WERE YOU DOING?

WHERE WERE YOU?

WHO WAS THERE?

COLORS

SMELLS

TEXTURES

SOUNDS

TASTES

FILL OUT THESE CLOUDS AS YOU THINK OF HAPPY MEMORIES. USE
THEM WHEN YOUR EMOTIONS BECOME OVERWHELMING.

NOTES

IMAGINATION PAGE

TITLE OF SPACE ____

SKETCH YOUR SAFE SPACE HERE:

WORDS THAT DESCRIBE YOUR SPACE:

SOUNDS

SIGHTS

SMELLS

TEXTURES

PEOPLE AND ANIMALS PRESENT

DATE:

TITLE OF SPACE --

SKETCH YOUR SAFE SPACE HERE:

WORDS THAT DESCRIBE YOUR SPACE:

SOUNDS

SIGHTS

SMELLS

TEXTURES

**PEOPLE AND
ANIMALS PRESENT**

WHAT WERE YOU DOING?

WHERE WERE YOU?

WHO WAS THERE?

COLORS

SMELLS

TEXTURES

SOUNDS

TASTES

FILL OUT THESE CLOUDS AS YOU THINK OF HAPPY MEMORIES. USE
THEM WHEN YOUR EMOTIONS BECOME OVERWHELMING.

NOTES

IMAGINATION PAGE

DATE:

TITLE OF SPACE --

SKETCH YOUR SAFE SPACE HERE:

WORDS THAT DESCRIBE YOUR SPACE:

SOUNDS

SIGHTS

SMELLS

TEXTURES

PEOPLE AND ANIMALS PRESENT

DATE:

TITLE OF SPACE --

SKETCH YOUR SAFE SPACE HERE:

WORDS THAT DESCRIBE YOUR SPACE:

SOUNDS

SIGHTS

SMELLS

TEXTURES

PEOPLE AND ANIMALS PRESENT

WHAT WERE YOU DOING?

WHERE WERE YOU?

WHO WAS THERE?

COLORS

SMELLS

TEXTURES

SOUNDS

TASTES

FILL OUT THESE CLOUDS AS YOU THINK OF HAPPY MEMORIES. USE
THEM WHEN YOUR EMOTIONS BECOME OVERWHELMING.

NOTES

IMAGINATION PAGE

TITLE OF SPACE

SKETCH YOUR SAFE SPACE HERE:

WORDS THAT DESCRIBE YOUR SPACE:

SOUNDS

SIGHTS

SMELLS

TEXTURES

PEOPLE AND ANIMALS PRESENT

TITLE OF SPACE --

SKETCH YOUR SAFE SPACE HERE:

WORDS THAT DESCRIBE YOUR SPACE:

SOUNDS

SIGHTS

SMELLS

TEXTURES

PEOPLE AND ANIMALS PRESENT

WHAT WERE YOU DOING?

WHERE WERE YOU?

WHO WAS THERE?

COLORS

SMELLS

TEXTURES

SOUNDS

TASTES

FILL OUT THESE CLOUDS AS YOU THINK OF HAPPY MEMORIES. USE
THEM WHEN YOUR EMOTIONS BECOME OVERWHELMING.

NOTES

IMAGINATION PAGE

DATE:

TITLE OF SPACE --

SKETCH YOUR SAFE SPACE HERE:

WORDS THAT DESCRIBE YOUR SPACE:

SOUNDS

SIGHTS

SMELLS

TEXTURES

PEOPLE AND ANIMALS PRESENT

DATE:

TITLE OF SPACE ____

SKETCH YOUR SAFE SPACE HERE:

WORDS THAT DESCRIBE YOUR SPACE:

SOUNDS

SIGHTS

SMELLS

TEXTURES

PEOPLE AND ANIMALS PRESENT

DATE:

WHAT WERE YOU DOING?

WHERE WERE YOU?

WHO WAS THERE?

COLORS

SMELLS

TEXTURES

SOUNDS

TASTES

FILL OUT THESE CLOUDS AS YOU THINK OF HAPPY MEMORIES. USE
THEM WHEN YOUR EMOTIONS BECOME OVERWHELMING.

NOTES

IMAGINATION PAGE

DATE:

TITLE OF SPACE ______________________________

SKETCH YOUR SAFE SPACE HERE:

WORDS THAT DESCRIBE YOUR SPACE:

SOUNDS

SIGHTS

SMELLS

TEXTURES

PEOPLE AND ANIMALS PRESENT

DATE:

TITLE OF SPACE

SKETCH YOUR SAFE SPACE HERE:

WORDS THAT DESCRIBE YOUR SPACE:

SOUNDS

SIGHTS

SMELLS

TEXTURES

PEOPLE AND ANIMALS PRESENT

WHAT WERE YOU DOING?

WHERE WERE YOU?

WHO WAS THERE?

COLORS

SMELLS

TEXTURES

SOUNDS

TASTES

FILL OUT THESE CLOUDS AS YOU THINK OF HAPPY MEMORIES. USE THEM WHEN YOUR EMOTIONS BECOME OVERWHELMING.

NOTES

IMAGINATION PAGE

DATE:

TITLE OF SPACE --

SKETCH YOUR SAFE SPACE HERE:

WORDS THAT DESCRIBE YOUR SPACE:

SOUNDS

SIGHTS

SMELLS

TEXTURES

PEOPLE AND ANIMALS PRESENT

DATE:

TITLE OF SPACE --

SKETCH YOUR SAFE SPACE HERE:

WORDS THAT DESCRIBE YOUR SPACE:

SOUNDS

SIGHTS

SMELLS

TEXTURES

PEOPLE AND ANIMALS PRESENT

DATE:

WHAT WERE YOU DOING?

WHERE WERE YOU?

WHO WAS THERE?

COLORS

SMELLS

TEXTURES

TASTES

SOUNDS

FILL OUT THESE CLOUDS AS YOU THINK OF HAPPY MEMORIES. USE
THEM WHEN YOUR EMOTIONS BECOME OVERWHELMING.

IMAGINATION PAGE

TITLE OF SPACE ---

SKETCH YOUR SAFE SPACE HERE:

WORDS THAT DESCRIBE YOUR SPACE:

SOUNDS

SIGHTS

SMELLS

TEXTURES

PEOPLE AND ANIMALS PRESENT

TITLE OF SPACE --

SKETCH YOUR SAFE SPACE HERE:

WORDS THAT DESCRIBE YOUR SPACE:

SOUNDS

SIGHTS

SMELLS

TEXTURES

PEOPLE AND ANIMALS PRESENT

DATE:

WHAT WERE YOU DOING?

WHERE WERE YOU?

WHO WAS THERE?

COLORS

SMELLS

TEXTURES

SOUNDS

TASTES

FILL OUT THESE CLOUDS AS YOU THINK OF HAPPY MEMORIES. USE
THEM WHEN YOUR EMOTIONS BECOME OVERWHELMING.

NOTES

IMAGINATION PAGE

TITLE OF SPACE --

SKETCH YOUR SAFE SPACE HERE:

WORDS THAT DESCRIBE YOUR SPACE:

SOUNDS

SIGHTS

SMELLS

TEXTURES

**PEOPLE AND
ANIMALS PRESENT**

TITLE OF SPACE ____

SKETCH YOUR SAFE SPACE HERE:

WORDS THAT DESCRIBE YOUR SPACE:

SOUNDS

SIGHTS

SMELLS

TEXTURES

PEOPLE AND ANIMALS PRESENT

DATE:

WHAT WERE YOU DOING?

WHERE WERE YOU?

WHO WAS THERE?

COLORS

SMELLS

TEXTURES

TASTES

SOUNDS

FILL OUT THESE CLOUDS AS YOU THINK OF HAPPY MEMORIES. USE
THEM WHEN YOUR EMOTIONS BECOME OVERWHELMING.

IMAGINATION PAGE

TITLE OF SPACE --

SKETCH YOUR SAFE SPACE HERE:

WORDS THAT DESCRIBE YOUR SPACE:

SOUNDS

SIGHTS

SMELLS

TEXTURES

PEOPLE AND ANIMALS PRESENT

TITLE OF SPACE ....

SKETCH YOUR SAFE SPACE HERE:

WORDS THAT DESCRIBE YOUR SPACE:

SOUNDS

SIGHTS

SMELLS

TEXTURES

PEOPLE AND ANIMALS PRESENT

DATE:

WHAT WERE YOU DOING?

WHERE WERE YOU?

WHO WAS THERE?

COLORS

SMELLS

TEXTURES

SOUNDS

TASTES

FILL OUT THESE CLOUDS AS YOU THINK OF HAPPY MEMORIES. USE
THEM WHEN YOUR EMOTIONS BECOME OVERWHELMING.

NOTES

DATE:

TITLE OF SPACE ________________________________

SKETCH YOUR SAFE SPACE HERE:

WORDS THAT DESCRIBE YOUR SPACE:

SOUNDS

SIGHTS

SMELLS

TEXTURES

PEOPLE AND ANIMALS PRESENT

TITLE OF SPACE

DATE:

SKETCH YOUR SAFE SPACE HERE:

WORDS THAT DESCRIBE YOUR SPACE:

SOUNDS

SIGHTS

SMELLS

TEXTURES

PEOPLE AND ANIMALS PRESENT

DATE:

WHAT WERE YOU DOING?

WHERE WERE YOU?

WHO WAS THERE?

COLORS

SMELLS

TEXTURES

TASTES

SOUNDS

FILL OUT THESE CLOUDS AS YOU THINK OF HAPPY MEMORIES. USE
THEM WHEN YOUR EMOTIONS BECOME OVERWHELMING.

IMAGINATION PAGE

TITLE OF SPACE --

SKETCH YOUR SAFE SPACE HERE:

WORDS THAT DESCRIBE YOUR SPACE:

SOUNDS

SIGHTS

SMELLS

TEXTURES

PEOPLE AND ANIMALS PRESENT

TITLE OF SPACE --

SKETCH YOUR SAFE SPACE HERE:

WORDS THAT DESCRIBE YOUR SPACE:

SOUNDS

SIGHTS

SMELLS

TEXTURES

PEOPLE AND ANIMALS PRESENT

WHAT WERE YOU DOING?

WHERE WERE YOU?

WHO WAS THERE?

COLORS

SMELLS

TEXTURES

SOUNDS

TASTES

FILL OUT THESE CLOUDS AS YOU THINK OF HAPPY MEMORIES. USE
THEM WHEN YOUR EMOTIONS BECOME OVERWHELMING.

NOTES

IMAGINATION PAGE

IMAGINATION PAGE

TITLE OF SPACE ....

SKETCH YOUR SAFE SPACE HERE:

WORDS THAT DESCRIBE YOUR SPACE:

SOUNDS

SIGHTS

SMELLS

TEXTURES

PEOPLE AND ANIMALS PRESENT

DATE:

TITLE OF SPACE ____

SKETCH YOUR SAFE SPACE HERE:

WORDS THAT DESCRIBE YOUR SPACE:

SOUNDS

SIGHTS

SMELLS

TEXTURES

PEOPLE AND ANIMALS PRESENT

DATE:

WHAT WERE YOU DOING?

WHERE WERE YOU?

WHO WAS THERE?

COLORS

SMELLS

TEXTURES

SOUNDS

TASTES

FILL OUT THESE CLOUDS AS YOU THINK OF HAPPY MEMORIES. USE
THEM WHEN YOUR EMOTIONS BECOME OVERWHELMING.

NOTES

IMAGINATION PAGE

IMAGINATION PAGE

DATE:

TITLE OF SPACE --

SKETCH YOUR SAFE SPACE HERE:

WORDS THAT DESCRIBE YOUR SPACE:

SOUNDS

SIGHTS

SMELLS

TEXTURES

PEOPLE AND ANIMALS PRESENT

DATE:

TITLE OF SPACE --

SKETCH YOUR SAFE SPACE HERE:

WORDS THAT DESCRIBE YOUR SPACE:

SOUNDS

SIGHTS

SMELLS

TEXTURES

PEOPLE AND ANIMALS PRESENT

WHAT WERE YOU DOING?

WHERE WERE YOU?

WHO WAS THERE?

COLORS

SMELLS

TEXTURES

SOUNDS

TASTES

FILL OUT THESE CLOUDS AS YOU THINK OF HAPPY MEMORIES. USE THEM WHEN YOUR EMOTIONS BECOME OVERWHELMING.

NOTES

IMAGINATION PAGE
IMAGINATION PAGE

DATE:

TITLE OF SPACE

SKETCH YOUR SAFE SPACE HERE:

WORDS THAT DESCRIBE YOUR SPACE:

SOUNDS

SIGHTS

SMELLS

TEXTURES

PEOPLE AND ANIMALS PRESENT

TITLE OF SPACE

SKETCH YOUR SAFE SPACE HERE:

WORDS THAT DESCRIBE YOUR SPACE:

SOUNDS

SIGHTS

SMELLS

TEXTURES

PEOPLE AND ANIMALS PRESENT

DATE:

WHAT WERE YOU DOING?

WHERE WERE YOU?

WHO WAS THERE?

COLORS

SMELLS

TEXTURES

TASTES

SOUNDS

FILL OUT THESE CLOUDS AS YOU THINK OF HAPPY MEMORIES. USE
THEM WHEN YOUR EMOTIONS BECOME OVERWHELMING.

NOTES

IMAGINATION PAGE

DATE:

TITLE OF SPACE --

SKETCH YOUR SAFE SPACE HERE:

WORDS THAT DESCRIBE YOUR SPACE:

SOUNDS

SIGHTS

SMELLS

TEXTURES

PEOPLE AND ANIMALS PRESENT

DATE:

TITLE OF SPACE --

SKETCH YOUR SAFE SPACE HERE:

WORDS THAT DESCRIBE YOUR SPACE:

SOUNDS

SIGHTS

SMELLS

TEXTURES

PEOPLE AND ANIMALS PRESENT

DATE:

WHAT WERE YOU DOING?

WHERE WERE YOU?

WHO WAS THERE?

COLORS

SMELLS

TEXTURES

SOUNDS

TASTES

FILL OUT THESE CLOUDS AS YOU THINK OF HAPPY MEMORIES. USE
THEM WHEN YOUR EMOTIONS BECOME OVERWHELMING.

NOTES

TITLE OF SPACE --

SKETCH YOUR SAFE SPACE HERE:

WORDS THAT DESCRIBE YOUR SPACE:

SOUNDS

SIGHTS

SMELLS

TEXTURES

**PEOPLE AND
ANIMALS PRESENT**

TITLE OF SPACE ____

SKETCH YOUR SAFE SPACE HERE:

WORDS THAT DESCRIBE YOUR SPACE:

SOUNDS

SIGHTS

SMELLS

TEXTURES

PEOPLE AND ANIMALS PRESENT

DATE:

WHAT WERE YOU DOING?

WHERE WERE YOU?

WHO WAS THERE?

COLORS

SMELLS

TEXTURES

SOUNDS

TASTES

FILL OUT THESE CLOUDS AS YOU THINK OF HAPPY MEMORIES. USE
THEM WHEN YOUR EMOTIONS BECOME OVERWHELMING.

IMAGINATION PAGE

TITLE OF SPACE --

SKETCH YOUR SAFE SPACE HERE:

WORDS THAT DESCRIBE YOUR SPACE:

SOUNDS

SIGHTS

SMELLS

TEXTURES

PEOPLE AND ANIMALS PRESENT

TITLE OF SPACE --

SKETCH YOUR SAFE SPACE HERE:

WORDS THAT DESCRIBE YOUR SPACE:

SOUNDS

SIGHTS

SMELLS

TEXTURES

PEOPLE AND ANIMALS PRESENT

WHAT WERE YOU DOING?

WHERE WERE YOU?

WHO WAS THERE?

COLORS

SMELLS

TEXTURES

SOUNDS

TASTES

FILL OUT THESE CLOUDS AS YOU THINK OF HAPPY MEMORIES. USE
THEM WHEN YOUR EMOTIONS BECOME OVERWHELMING.

NOTES

IMAGINATION PAGE

DATE:

TITLE OF SPACE

SKETCH YOUR SAFE SPACE HERE:

WORDS THAT DESCRIBE YOUR SPACE:

SOUNDS

SIGHTS

SMELLS

TEXTURES

PEOPLE AND ANIMALS PRESENT

DATE:

TITLE OF SPACE --

SKETCH YOUR SAFE SPACE HERE:

WORDS THAT DESCRIBE YOUR SPACE:

SOUNDS

SIGHTS

SMELLS

TEXTURES

PEOPLE AND ANIMALS PRESENT

DATE:

WHAT WERE YOU DOING?

WHERE WERE YOU?

WHO WAS THERE?

COLORS

SMELLS

TEXTURES

TASTES

SOUNDS

FILL OUT THESE CLOUDS AS YOU THINK OF HAPPY MEMORIES. USE
THEM WHEN YOUR EMOTIONS BECOME OVERWHELMING.

NOTES

IMAGINATION PAGE

IMAGINATION PAGE

TITLE OF SPACE --

SKETCH YOUR SAFE SPACE HERE:

WORDS THAT DESCRIBE YOUR SPACE:

SOUNDS

SIGHTS

SMELLS

TEXTURES

PEOPLE AND
ANIMALS PRESENT

DATE:

TITLE OF SPACE

SKETCH YOUR SAFE SPACE HERE:

WORDS THAT DESCRIBE YOUR SPACE:

SOUNDS

SIGHTS

SMELLS

TEXTURES

PEOPLE AND ANIMALS PRESENT

WHAT WERE YOU DOING?

WHERE WERE YOU?

WHO WAS THERE?

COLORS

SMELLS

TEXTURES

SOUNDS

TASTES

FILL OUT THESE CLOUDS AS YOU THINK OF HAPPY MEMORIES. USE THEM WHEN YOUR EMOTIONS BECOME OVERWHELMING.

NOTES

IMAGINATION PAGE
IMAGINATION PAGE

TITLE OF SPACE ---

SKETCH YOUR SAFE SPACE HERE:

WORDS THAT DESCRIBE YOUR SPACE:

SOUNDS

SIGHTS

SMELLS

TEXTURES

**PEOPLE AND
ANIMALS PRESENT**

DATE:

TITLE OF SPACE ____

SKETCH YOUR SAFE SPACE HERE:

WORDS THAT DESCRIBE YOUR SPACE:

SOUNDS

SIGHTS

SMELLS

TEXTURES

PEOPLE AND ANIMALS PRESENT